SQUANTO

and the

MIRACLE OF THANKSGIVING

ERIC METAXAS

ILLUSTRATED BY SHANNON STIRNWEIS

Tommy
NELSON®

Thomas Nelson, Inc.
Nashville

To Annerose Mary Regina,
another of God's miracles worthy of thanksgiving

Text © 1999 by Eric Metaxas.
Illustrations © 1999 by Shannon Stirnweis.

All rights reserved. No portion of this book may be reproduced in any form without the written permission of the publisher, except for brief excerpts in reviews.

Published in Nashville, Tennessee, by Tommy Nelson ®, a division of Thomas Nelson, Inc.

Library of Congress Cataloging-in-Publication Data
Metaxas, Eric.
  Squanto and the miracle of Thanksgiving / by Eric Metaxas ;
illustrated by Shannon Stirnweis.
    p.   cm.
  Summary: Describes how the Massachusetts Indian Squanto was
captured by the British, sold into slavery in Spain, and ultimately
returned to the New World to become a guide and friend for the
Pilgrims.
  ISBN 0-8499-5864-4
  1. Squanto Juvenile literature. 2. Wampanoag Indians Biography
Juvenile literature. 3. Pilgrims (New Plymouth Colony) Juvenile
literature. 4. Thanksgiving Day Juvenile literature. [1. Squanto.
2. Wampanoag Indians Biography. 3. Indians of North America—
Massachusetts Biography. 4. Pilgrims (New Plymouth Colony)
5. Thanksgiving Day.]   I. Stirnweis, Shannon, ill. II. Title.
E99.W2S645 1999
974.4004'973— dc21   99-22912
                                                      CIP

Printed in the United States of America
  7 8 9 LB 08 07 06 05

Every once in a great while, the hand of God is easy to see, and for a brief moment, fairy tales and history are the same thing. This story is about one of those times.

It was in the year of our Lord 1608. Few white men had ever seen North America. But everywhere there were various tribes of natives, some who were friendly and trusting, others who were fierce and cruel.

On the chilly, gray coast of what is today called Massachusetts, there lived a tribe called the Patuxets, who were as friendly and trusting as any that lived. One of them, a boy of about twelve, was called Tisquantum, or Squanto.

One day while Squanto and some other Patuxet braves were hunting for lobsters along the shore, they saw a giant vessel. It was the size of a hundred canoes! The men aboard it wore strange clothing and had hair on their faces like fur!

But Squanto was not frightened. He had heard of such men. "These are the men who come every few years from the world across the water," Squanto told his friends. "They have come to trade with us."

Squanto knew that they often brought bright beads, glinting knives, ax heads, and iron pots to exchange for animal pelts and furs. "Let's see what they have brought!" Squanto said. And he and his companions excitedly raced down to the water.

At first the men seemed friendly to the young braves and offered them food. But then, without warning, the men attacked! They grabbed the trusting Patuxets and threw them to the ground, tying stiff ropes around their wrists and feet. Squanto had never been so frightened! The men dragged the braves to their giant ship and threw them into the dark hold beneath the ship's deck, laughing all the while. Then they locked the hatch above.

Squanto shivered in the darkness. The ropes hurt his wrists and ankles. The ship began to move, and Squanto did not know where he was going, or indeed, if he would ever see sunlight again. *Why had these men done this?* Squanto listened to the water lapping against the hull of the ship. Somehow he knew that he was leaving the world of his childhood forever.

Days passed, and then weeks. They had traveled for so long that it seemed to Squanto they must now be on the other side of the sky, behind the moon and sun and stars. *Where were they going?*

Then one day the ship dropped anchor. At long last they had come to land. The hatch was opened, and Squanto and his fellow captives were brought ashore. The glaring sun burned their eyes; the air was dry and hot; and everything was dusty from the great heat. Squanto did not know it yet, but he was now in the country of Spain, in a city called Málaga.

One of the men from the ship roughly herded Squanto and the other braves toward a crowd of people on the dock. One by one, the braves were forced to stand before the jeering crowd. They were being sold as slaves! Squanto watched his companions as each one was sold and taken away forever.

But God had another plan for Squanto. On the dock that morning stood a group of men who were different from the others. These men were called monks, and they served God. When it was Squanto's turn to be sold, one of the monks held up a small bag of heavy coins. A man from the ship snatched the coins and shoved Squanto toward the monks.

As the monks led Squanto to the monastery where they
lived, they spoke kindly to him in words Squanto could not
understand. The monks fed Squanto, gave him a comfortable
place to sleep, and helped him understand that they meant
him no harm.

As time passed, the monks taught Squanto their language
and about their faith. They explained that the God they

worshiped saw everything that had ever happened. "He knows the future as well as the past," the monks explained. "And all the people in the world are God's children."

"God loves you," they said, "and He has seen all you have been through. If you will trust Him, He will use those difficulties in ways you could never imagine."

The monks knew that Squanto missed his family, so they tried to help him find a way to go back home to America. Finally, they came upon a good plan. But first, Squanto would have to travel all the way to England. That's where the trading ships were that sometimes sailed across the great Atlantic Ocean to Squanto's home.

So about five years after Squanto had first arrived in Spain, the time finally came for him to leave. He bid the dear monks farewell and traveled northward in a ship to London, England.

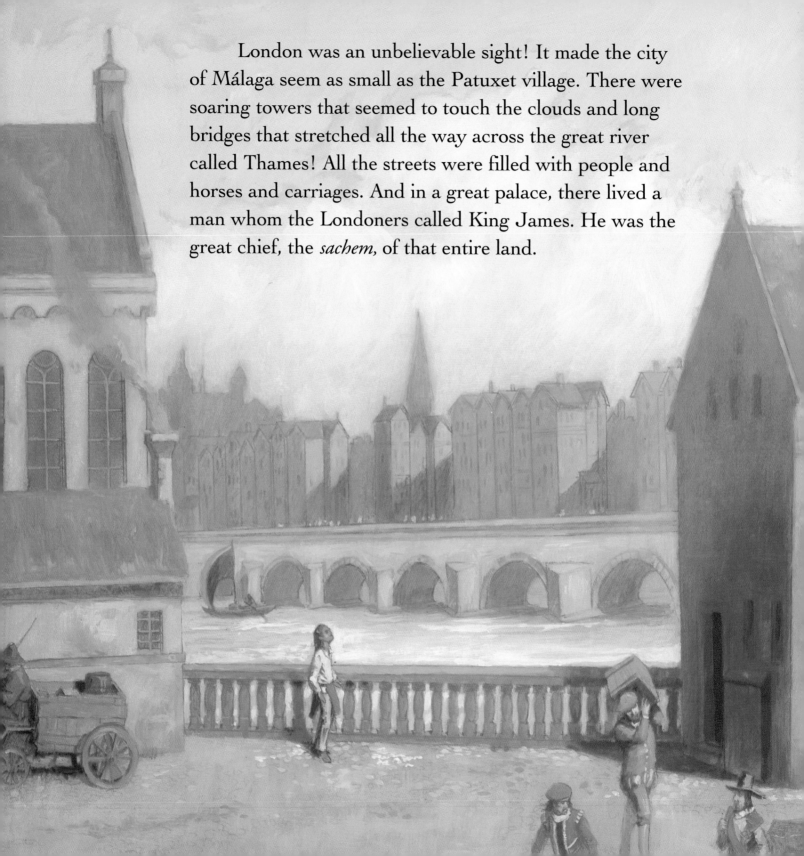

London was an unbelievable sight! It made the city of Málaga seem as small as the Patuxet village. There were soaring towers that seemed to touch the clouds and long bridges that stretched all the way across the great river called Thames! All the streets were filled with people and horses and carriages. And in a great palace, there lived a man whom the Londoners called King James. He was the great chief, the *sachem,* of that entire land.

The monks had sent Squanto to the home of a London merchant named John Slanie. After hearing Squanto's story, Slanie and his family welcomed Squanto into their home. "As soon as I find another ship headed for America," Slanie promised, "you will be on it, Squanto."

Squanto's heart leaped. He was going home!

"But it might be a long while before such a ship is found," Slanie warned. "Until then, you will stay here with us. We will teach you our language and our ways. Perhaps you will be able to pay your passage back to America by working as a translator on one of the trading ships."

Squanto sighed heavily, but at least now there was hope. He would stay in London with the Slanies and work in their stables until a ship was found that would carry him home.

At last, five long years later, in the year 1618, a
ship was found. Squanto could hardly believe it. It had
been ten years since he had been kidnapped from Patuxet
as a boy of twelve. At long last he was going home!

With tears in his eyes, Squanto bid farewell to the Slanies and
to the great city of London with all its towers and bridges. Then
Squanto boarded the ship and sailed westward, toward America.

Far across the Atlantic Ocean, the ship stopped in
Newfoundland at a large trading post, where it would remain until
spring. Again Squanto waited.

When at last spring arrived, Squanto boarded the ship one
more time. As the many days passed, Squanto thought back
over the last ten years. Had he imagined them? Was he
really going home?

Then one day, as Squanto stood peering across the waters, he saw land!

"Land ho!" he yelled. *"Hurrah!"*

As the ship drew closer, Squanto saw that he was not far from where he had been kidnapped all those years ago. *Home!*

Squanto went ashore and immediately began running toward his village. But something was wrong! The fields around the village were empty and untended. There was no one on the path to greet him.

When he reached the village, there wasn't a soul to be seen.
Not even a dog barked at his arrival. What had happened? Worried
and confused, Squanto walked to the village of a neighboring tribe
some miles away.

There Squanto learned the terrible news. While he had been
away, a terrible illness had struck. His whole village had become
sick. No one had survived! This news was more than Squanto could
bear. Had his years of exile and his long journey back been for
nothing? *How could God allow this to happen?*

For a time Squanto lived with this neighboring tribe. But as he watched the happy families all around him, his sadness only grew. Finally, he went to live in the woods by himself. There, Squanto sat, listening to the wind and to the birds singing in the swaying trees. As he pondered the great sorrow in his heart, he talked to God.

When the trees began to bud again, a tribesman from another village came to visit Squanto. His name was Samoset, and he told an amazing story. The year before, a shipload of families had come and settled in Patuxet—in the very place where Squanto had lived as a boy. Samoset told Squanto he must come and see them. Squanto agreed.

When Squanto came to the edge of what had once been his
village, he marveled at the changes that had been made. Then he
saw them—English people! They spoke and dressed just like those

who had been so kind to him in London. Squanto rejoiced to see children again playing on the land where he himself had played!

Squanto approached the English people and began speaking to them in their own language. "Good morning!" he called. "My name is Squanto!" The English were so amazed that they could not speak. How did this native know their language so well?

Then Squanto told them the sad story of his kidnapping, of his time in Spain and London, and of his long journey home. Then the English people told Squanto of their own search for a home.

Because these people, who were called Pilgrims, chose to worship God differently from other English people, many of them had been arrested and thrown into jail! So they had left England and traveled to Holland, where they lived for several years. But when the Pilgrims saw that their children were forgetting the English ways and were picking up the habits of the new country,

the Pilgrims decided to travel across the ocean to the New World. They trusted that God would lead them to a new home.

"And God led us to this very spot," one of the Pilgrims said. "We have named it Plymouth, in honor of the town in England where we once lived."

Then they told Squanto about the terrible first winter in their new home. Half of them had died from sickness and starvation.

"We didn't have time to build proper houses," they explained. "The winds were bitter, and the cold came in through the cracks in our huts. Many of us were already sick and weak from the long journey across the ocean. And then, there wasn't enough food . . ."

As the Pilgrims told their story, the sorrow in their voices broke Squanto's heart. He knew what it was like to lose loved ones!

William Bradford, the governor of Plymouth, then spoke. "It is like the story of Joseph from our sacred Scriptures," he said. "Like you, Joseph was also taken from his home and sold as a slave. But God had a plan for him. Through Joseph, God was able to save many people from starving. What man had intended for evil, God intended for good." Then Bradford smiled at Squanto. "Perhaps God has sent you to be our Joseph," he said.

In the weeks that followed, Squanto felt like a child again.
It was so good to see his village filled with people.

The Pilgrims worked hard to learn the ways of their new
home. Squanto showed them how to plant corn by burying three
kernels along with a fish for fertilizer. He taught them how to find
and catch eels in the muddy streams. And he showed them the best
places to look for lobsters among the sea rocks.

When autumn came, the Pilgrims decided to set aside a time to thank God for His merciful blessings. They invited Squanto and the other braves from Samoset's tribe to join them.

When the great day came, ninety warriors appeared from the forest, carrying deer, wild turkeys, and all manner of vegetables. This would be a great feast!

When everyone was seated, Governor Bradford began to pray: "Thank You, Lord, for sending Squanto to us," he prayed. "We know that Your hand has been on him through all of his trials, and that You have prepared him to be our guide and our friend in a time of great need. Squanto is Your living answer to our tears and prayers."

And in his heart, Squanto also thanked God for the Pilgrims, for they had shown Squanto that God really had used him as part of His great plan, just as the Spanish monks had said so many years before.

Hallelujah! Who but the glorious God of heaven could so miraculously weave together the wandering lives of a lonely Patuxet brave and a struggling band of English Pilgrims in such a way that would bless the whole world for centuries to come?

*So this Thanksgiving,
when you thank God
for all He has given you,
remember to thank Him
for Squanto, the Patuxet brave
who was God's wonderful gift
to America in the
rosy dawn of its history.*